Carcharhinus plumbeus

Zachary Webb Nicholls

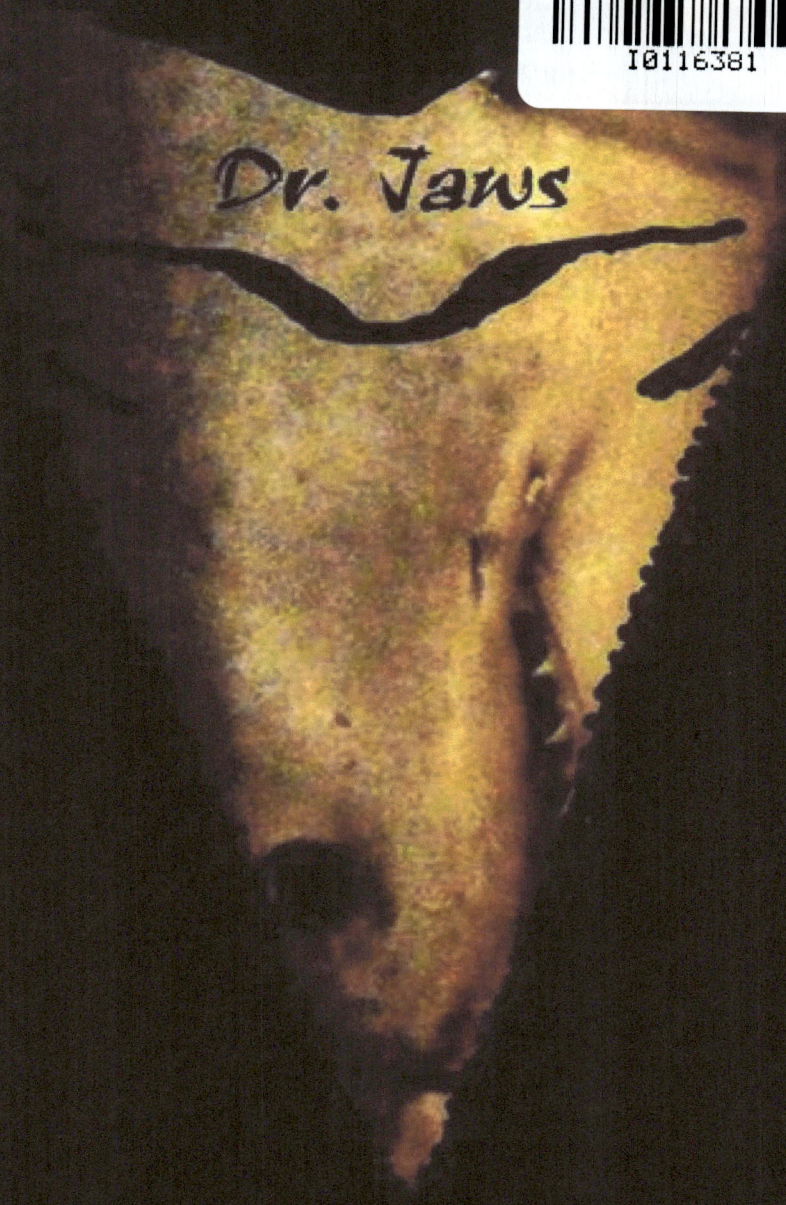

Dr. Jaws

Carcharhinus plumbeus
Copyright © 2014 by Zachary Webb Nicholls (Dr. Jaws)

All rights reserved. Published in the United States by Deep Sea Publishing LLC, Herndon, Virginia.

ISBN-13: 978-1-939535-61-0
ISBN: 1939535611
E-Book ISBN-13: 978-1-939535-62-7
E-Book ISBN: 193953562X

www.deepseapublishing.com

Printed in the United States of America

Hello friend,

What you are about to read is secret.

Each word, picture, and symbol has a meaning, and together they will help you find something very strange, but very exciting. Furthermore, each word, picture, and symbol is anchored in a living truth, but in order to fully understand what that truth is, you need to do some exploring.

Beyond this little book, there is a boundless, bountiful wealth of knowledge within your reach. You of course are not required to seek it, but if you do, I assure you will be rewarded with a richer understanding of our shark, the seas, and the mystery of life itself.

For now, you hold in your hands a map. Let it take you—from the past, to the present, to the weird—deep into an ocean of legends, of dark wonders, and of amber eyes...

....let it take you to Shark.

Carcharhinus
plumbeus

Little friend,

Cherished friend

Bright in smile and

warm in eyes

to you I am

a devoted fan

and with you time

forever flies

Starlight is finite
A star has a time to end
Explosive its death

Scattered star pieces
Combine into the combined
Birth of sun and earth

Sun fire creates
With calm earth, air, and water
Life elemental

~ *Domain Eukarya* ~

Imagine a mountain

Cool and calming

Trickling water down its slope

It is serene in its grey

Paint it with a domain

Of life so rich in color

That the eyes will forever wonder

At its design and sustain

A curiosity

Unique only to Eukarya

When cell within cell became cell itself

So long ago, a peak

In life was reached

From origins so humble

Came oranges so fiery

With jades, emeralds, and harlequins each

Beauties of the forest

Protecting the ambling reds

And boisterous blues

With calming arms best

Suited for shading

Amber-centered violets

And cinnabar-sighted mosaics

All art never fading

This domain is of color

See Eukarya

Splendid and diverse

Muses of the world

For the art that it is

~Kingdom Animalia~

Look what the dawn has broken
Something new stirs in the seas
A novel language now spoken
The animals have come to be

~

From one tiny sponge to one funny man
A simple life will always be banned
A drama that we cannot understand
The animals, come and play, come and play

A hardworking ant meets an unfriendly beetle

While two birds romance, it seems nothing's
sweeter

A seahorse's dance is such a unique love

Animals, come and play, come and play

~

Embrace the feeling of life

A body that's one from many

A hunger that sets you right

~

And chase in manner uncanny

Your strange sweet compassions

You animal, go and play, go and play

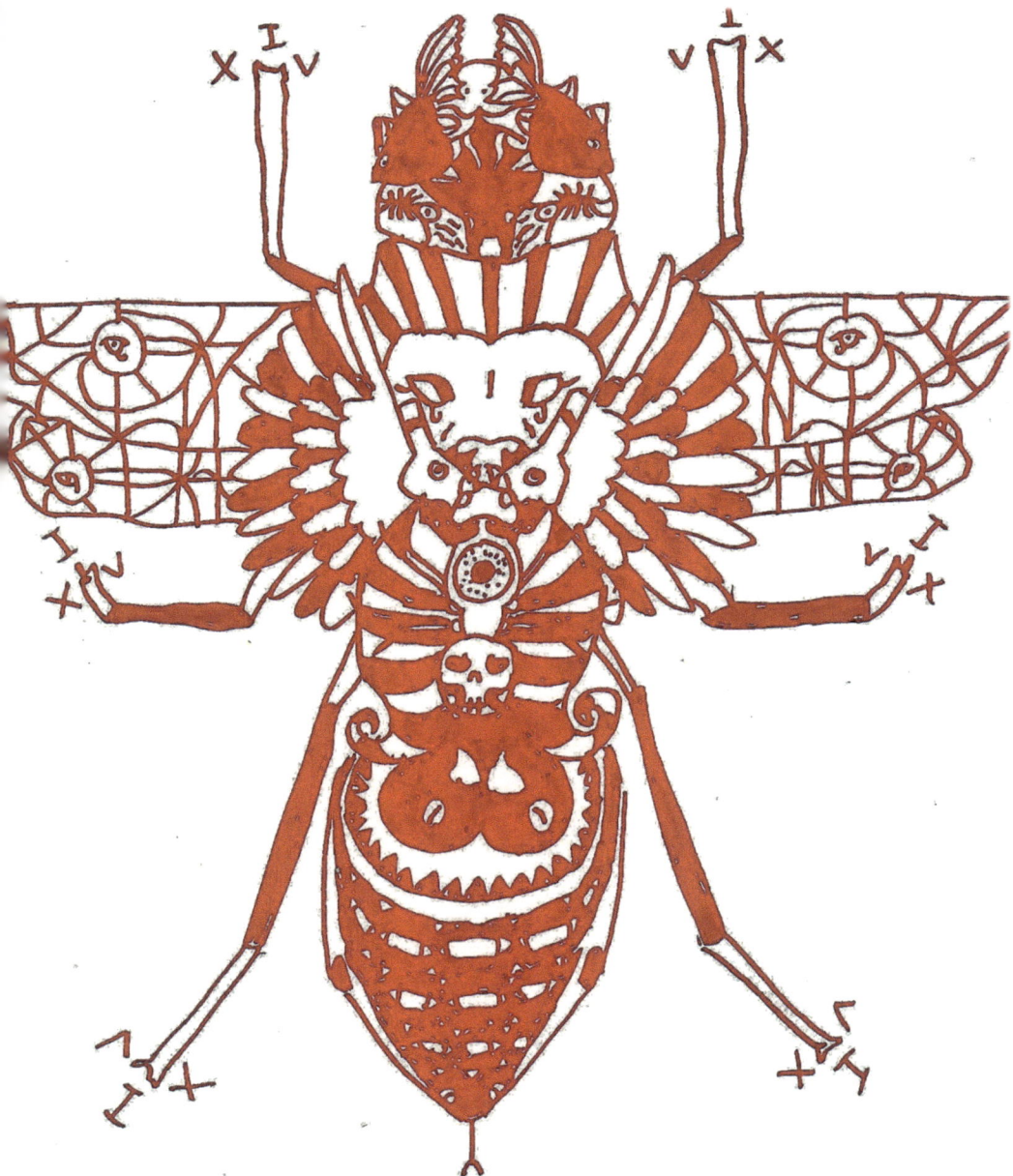

~Phylum Chordata~

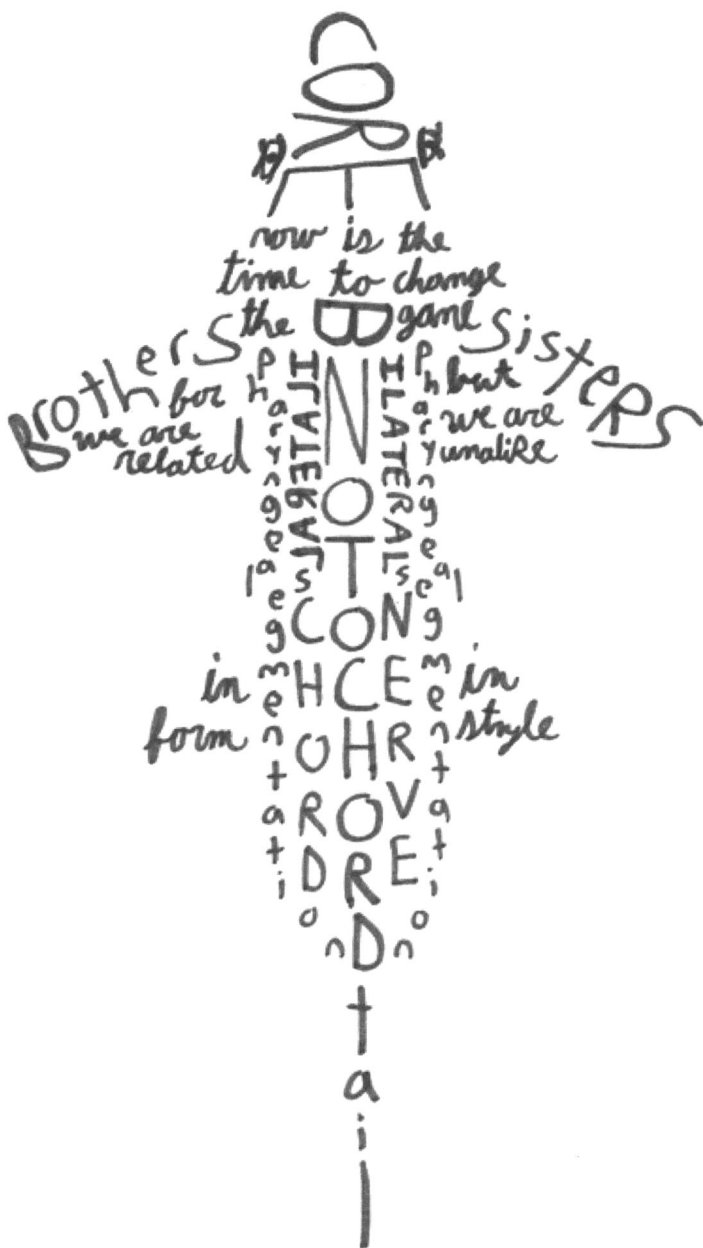

CORD

now is the
time to change
the game sisters

brothers for we are related but we are yunalike

NOTOCHORD
pharyngeal slits
bilateral symmetry

different in form
different in style

tail

~ *Class Chondrichthyes* ~

There is a hall of marble and limestone—of honor and ocean—adorned with obsidian shadows; the Chondrichthyan Silhouettes. Each Silhouette is an embodiment of form and essence, said to be constructed by the gods to remind the world of the Living Shadows; the chimaera, the ray, and the shark.

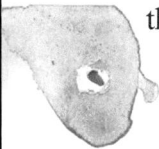

Believed to be guardians of both the ocean and the human soul, The Living Shadows served to consume the weaknesses of each. Through so doing, they culled corruption and protected the life of both soul and sea.

To honor this nobility cloaked in ferocity, the Chondrichthyan Silhouettes are each adorned with an eye of pearl and gemstone. Together, body and eye capture the essence of a Living Shadow:

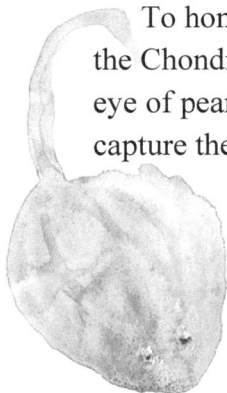

A power cooled with grace
An immortal who could die
A legend with a heartbeat.

~Order Carcharhiniformes~

Beauteous beasts of time
A standard and yet an ideal
Coasting beyond the sands
And into depths of teal

For fear they do not
As in their eyes reveal
An ancient secret light
Seen only by those who feel

Akin to their plight
And akin to their strength
A cutting edge of blue
A coursing blood of length

By such eyes as theirs
Which close upon a kill
They form their sacred forms
The fears that we've instilled

These rare and common types
Of shark will always be
As changing as the tides
But still masters of the sea

~Family Carcharhinidae~

The requiem sharks
Aqua volcanoes aware
Powerful but calm

~*Genus Carcharhinus*~

SHARPNOSE

"Teoso f rlksfdoq tl ao teo stnkdnqd senqhs; teoy nqo jlst fktoqtwfkod wfte eujnkfty, nkd nqo teo stuii lb iocokds."

Note: The above is a keyword cypher. The keyword is hidden on the following page. Use it to unlock a smaller insight.

The Leaden One

Nardo, 1827

Carcharhinus plumbeus

A medium-sized shark with an average mass of 70kg. It is distinguished by the very large 1st dorsal fin, large pectoral fins, and presence of an inter-dorsal ridge.

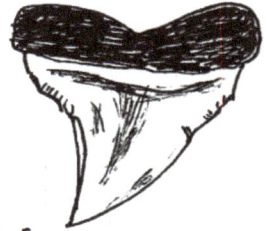

Sandbar Shark   Tiburón trozo

القرش الرملي   高鳍真鲨   メジロザメ

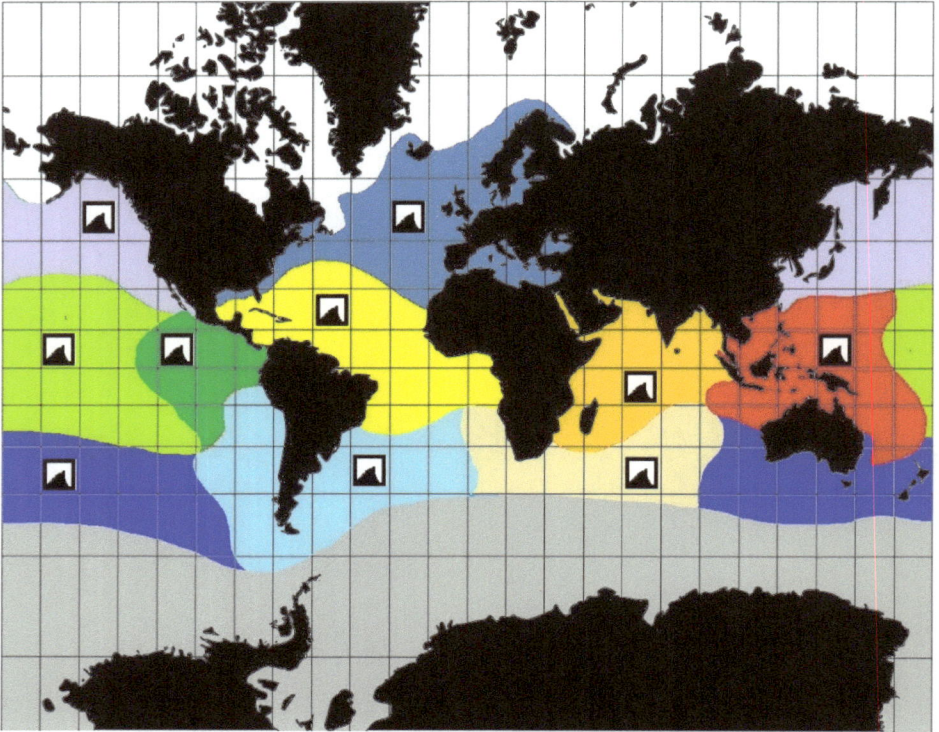

~Global Distribution~

North Akula Sea

Peaceful Sea of Mano

Tempest Requin Sea

Sunrise Sea of Tiburon

Wild Zame Sea

Grande Tubarao Sea

Sunset Sea of Reken

Groot Haai Sea

Colorful Sea of Sarka

Great Shark Sea

Bountiful Sea of Shayu

South Sarko Sea

~Haunts~

Carcharhinus plumbeus

can be found in the following zones:

Littoral   Neritic

Sunlit   Twilight

~

"Well, let's see, uhhh...ok, well, sometimes I swim alone, sometimes with the guys, eh, OH WAIT, we CAN'T swim with the big sharks. I mean, it's not a rule or anything... it's just a super bad idea as they pretty much want to eat us. SOOO SCARY, but its ok because I've got my bottom...uhh, my seabed, I mean...yeah, anyway I stick close to there and count the ripples that the tide presses into the sand...oh, and eat of course. Have you ever heard of flatfish? THEY'RE SO WEIRD, and yet so yummy..."

~ *Habits* ~

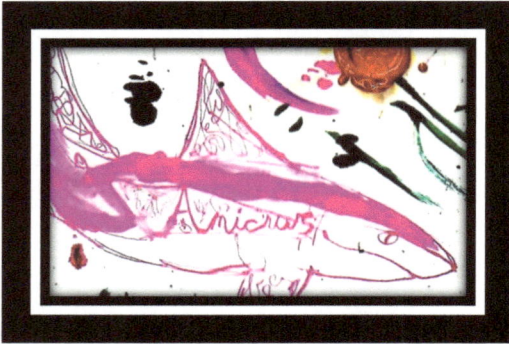

Carcharhinus plumbeus is a bit aggressive when it comes to mating. A male will follow a female and bite at her back until she swims upside-down to receive him. Females give birth after 8-12 months, and then take a 'break' lasting up to a year or two.

Carcharhinus plumbeus pups enjoy shallow inshore nursery areas along the coast and often form sex-segregated schools. The species grows slowly and matures late in life; this, in combination with the shark's slow reproductive rate, makes *Carcharhinus plumbeus* especially sensitive to fishing pressures.

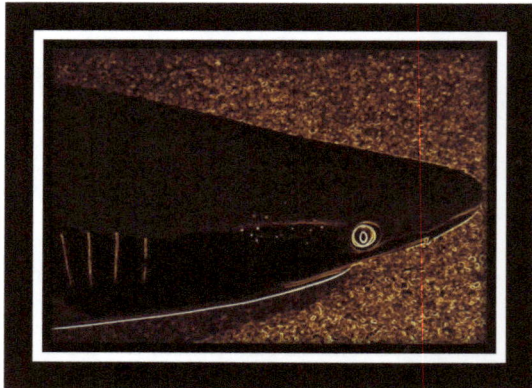

~ *Humanity* ~

Carcharhinus plumbeus is to be perceived as a

POTENTIALLY DANGEROUS SHARK

In light of the concerning attributes that follow:

Its proximity to man
Its fearsome dentition

These attributes are juxtaposed with the truth that

Carcharhinus plumbeus has been implicated in

VERY FEW UNPROVOKED ATTACKS

As a resource, the shark offers palatable meat and is a popular focus of public aquaria.

~

However, man has overfished Carcharhinus plumbeus, and furthermore subjected the shark to the cruelty of finning.

As a result, Carcharhinus plumbeus is a

VULNERABLE SPECIES

~ *Amicus* ~

"A tale about our shark, and more...."

Lizzie Brock was a petite, punctual, precocious pupil of public policy who presently was pissed at the potential problem of her possibly being prohibited a prominent position proffered at a much-pined-for pre-doctoral program.

Currently, she was fuming on a dock, chucking what pebbles she could find into the water as if they represented her troubles and what she'd like to do with them. She wasn't an angry person by any means, but rather someone who just HATED being overwhelmed... along with this current graduate school dilemma, Lizzie was dealing with minor family issues, major academic annoyances, and mediocre amounts of idiocy coming from the boys of her life.

It all could have been more easily dealt with if she had someone to talk to, but the sad truth remained that everyone in Lizzie's life was either studying abroad, generally busy, or just a moron. It had been quiet a lonely time recently, and judging from her currently depressed mood, it was starting to wear into her spirits.

In quite concentration she thought, 'EVERYONE ON THIS PLANET CAN GO KICK A BEAR, GET EATEN BY THAT BEAR, AND THEN GO TO BEAR-HELL WHERE THEY'LL BE PREPTUALLY EATEN BY MORE BEARS VENGEFUL FOR THE CRIMES AGAINST BOTH THE EARTHLY BEARS AND ME!', and most-angrily chucked the largest pebble into the water with a giant splash. Yes…she can be a bit dramatic…but her emotions were her emotions, and right now their current lack of a vent made any violent thought all the more reasonable.

"I just wished I had someone to talk to…" she mumbled aloud, and as she was about to chuck yet another pebble off the dock, she stopped to let those words sink in. It hurt being so alone…it hurt not feeling like she had any friends…it hurt not having absolutely anyone to listen to her, to walk her through these difficulties, offer her support…it just was, truly, sad.

Thinking more in this way, she started to cry…she was 22 and tough, and not really used to crying…but right now, alone on this dock at the edge of her world, she needed to fall apart.

"I just wished I had someone to talk to" she mumbled again, this time quite wetter. Determined to make it a mantra, she almost said it again, but was cut off by…

"TALK TO MEEEE!!!!"

A small, squat, but nonetheless terrifying shark popped its eager head out of the water, staring directly at Lizzie who, in this order: SCREAMED, shot a pebble squarely between the shark's eyes, fell over backwards, and lay paralyzed-by-fear onto the dock, all within a 5-second timeframe.

"Ouch!" The shark fell backwards into the water with a small plop.

For a good minute Lizzie did nothing but lay there, staring up into the sky with eyes wide in shock, questioning her sanity. 'Is it…is it just the heat?' she wondered. Rapidly she was replaying the situation; she DID see a face and she DID throw a pebble and something DID frighten her enough to be currently flat on her back like an inverted ladybug.

Accepting these facts, Lizzie let out a scratchy and barely audible, "heeeeellllp…"

"Come again?" A voice sounded to her left, beyond the edge of the dock, somewhere below. With neither her frozen expression nor paralyzed position changing, Lizzie said automatically, "I want help."

"Help with what?"

"…escape"

"Why?"

"I don't know".

"Ok, well…well you're silly!"

Shortly following this statement, a sizeable splash of water came up from the voice's side of the dock and fell promptly upon Lizzie's face. The cold, wet shock snapped her out of paralysis, and compelled her to roll over and look towards the sea. With newfound anger mixed with slight curiosity, Lizzie crawled ever so slowly away from her initial fears and inched closer to the edge.

'This has got to be a joke...' she thought with earnest, 'there is no such thing as a talking shark'.

When she arrived at the edge, she looked down, and saw that same sharky face which this time made a concentrated effort to smile. Lizzie's eyes grew wide again and she almost screamed, but the observant shark tried to counter this upcoming unpleasantness with an emphatic, "*Hiiiii!*"

The attempt turned out to be creepy.

"AHHHH!!!" Lizzie jumped back again with a loud shout, but the shark— now looking distressed—tried rapidly to reverse this situation.

"I'm sorry, I didn't mean to scare you! Umm, oh wait! Is this how you say, 'hello?' Um, AHHHHH!!!"

The shark panicked and so defaulted on mimicry. As a result, there were now two silly animals screaming at each other, only that one was seriously frightened, while the other was only an emphatic actor.

"STOP IT!" Lizzie shouted, now trying to seize some quiet sanity—she needed to get to the bottom of this. "STOP YELLING!"

The shark obeyed and watched intently. Lizzie took a few deep breaths and determinedly began her interrogation .

"Who are you?", she barked.

"Oh! Um…I don't know!"

"What do you mean you don't know? Do you have a name?"

"Uh...Is that a body part?"

It was apparently a wholehearted question. There was an audible silence followed by a deliberate, "No."

"Oh. Well...what is it?" The shark was now excited and wiggled a bit in anticipation. Lizzie for a split-second thought it was actually kind of cute, but her guard was still up.

"It's what we call each other" she said flatly, "it's how we say hello."

"Yay! Can I say hello?"

"Maybe...but first, WHY are you here? AND HOW CAN YOU TALK?"

"Well, I thought...I thought you wanted someone to talk to..." the little shark looked down and seemed a tiny bit hurt *"Certus sum, quomodo loqui didiceram..."*

"WAIT, WHAT? WHAAAT?! YOU SPEAK LATIN?!" Lizzie was now even more confused than ever, but she recognized the language. She herself loved Latin and was amazed to hear it for the first time outside of lecture…even though the speaker was a talking shark that could be the face of her apparent delirium.

"Oh, sorry, yes I do! I mean, etiam!"

"How?! How in the world do you speak Latin? OR ENGLISH!?"

"Nescio!"

Brilliant. The bilingual shark did not know how he became a bilingual shark. Or even a lingual shark.

"Um…well…" Lizzie was at first scrambling to make sense of ANYTHING that was happening right now…but to her surprise an old emotion slowly emerged and started to nestle deep within.

When she was little, Lizzie loved the idea of talking with animals…she loved to pretend with her dog Albert and interpret to her parents exactly what Albert needed…she loved to dream of traveling to distant places and meeting new kinds of birds, fish, and mammals who would tell her their life stories and opinions on being an animal…this childhood dream, this warm blanket of a concept that made her so happy when she was small…it was strangely, insanely, but excitingly being realized right now.

Bizarrely, against all her better judgment as a 22-year-old adult living in a logical, rational, sensible society…she honestly wanted to surrender to this moment, and partake in its fun.

"Um…do you want a name?" she asked, much more politely than before.

The shark instantly picked up on a positive change of mood and bobbed up and down with delight.

"*Yeah-yeah-yeah!*" he quickly squeaked

Lizzie's mouth twitched almost into a smile, and she calmly adjusted herself into a more comfortable wigwam position.

"Let's see…people sometimes are named after things they like or find interesting. Do yo—"

"*Squidmeat is interesting!*" the shark blurted out, and swam in circles of excitement.

"NO, you're not going to be called 'Squidmeat'." Lizzie almost laughed, and from this angle she could see that the shark was in fact rather small and a bit rotund. "Um…you know, Latin names are pretty…what do you think of something like, 'Nero'?"

"*Nope! He watched Rome burn.*" The shark said matter-of-factly.

"Wait, WHAT?! How in the worl-"

"*What about 'Amicus'?*" the shark excitedly interrupted. "*It's Latin for 'friend'!*"

"Yeah sure that's fine" Lizzie quickly answered, "but seriously, how—"

"*I can be 'Ami' for short!*"

"Oh my gosh…" Lizzie was getting slightly frustrated by Ami's apparently small attention-span, but the shark's enthusiasm was infectious, and yet again she could not help but laugh.

"Ok, ok, calm down…so your name is 'Ami'."

"*Yes!*"

"Great, it's nice to meet you. My name is Lizzie."

"Hi Lizzie! Why were you all leaky earlier?" Ami seemed more curious than concerned.

"Oh jeez". Lizzie was taken aback by this forward question and put her palm to her forehead. "You mean crying? You saw that?"

Ami noticed that Lizzie's mood changed ever so slightly into something bluer, and he quickly focused all of his attention onto her.

"Oh, I'm sorry...are you all right? I can be that someone you wanted to talk to!" he offered emphatically.

"Yeah, it's fine...I just have a lot going on right now."

"Well, I have zippo going on right now! So if we add your 'a lot' to my 'zippo'

and divide by two, then we get approximately half of 'a lot', which is 'a little', which is probably better, don't you think?"

He made zero sense. But it was adorable.

"Ok" Lizzie started to giggle, "Are you saying that you'd like to hear about it? Do you really want to get bored by my life-troubles?"

"Yes I do! Bring it!" the enthusiasm was back.

"Ok" she giggled again.

Lizzie told Ami everything that was on her mind: the graduate schools, the unending homework, her recent breakup, her family problems…and though he really didn't get half of it, it was still for her a bit of a catharsis. Her problems, when said aloud, actually didn't seem that bad anymore…she almost felt silly for being so gloomy earlier, and shared this thought with her newfound friend.

"It's ok, dude!" he piped reassuringly. *"We all get kind of down sometimes."*

"Yeah, I know…what brings you down?"

"Seeing a big shark that wants to eat me." He shuddered at this thought.

"Oh my! That…that would do it!" This concept of Ami facing such deadly ocean perils made Lizzie feel even sillier for her earlier woes.

"Yeah, OH MY GOSH, LIZZIE, THEY'RE SO BIG! Like…like 4 'Ami's big!"

"Oh no! Where are they? Do they li--

"What's your opinion on the spherical earth? Was Aristotle's 'De Caelo'

correct?" Ami's short attention-span returned with brilliance.

"This is nuts. Ami, HOW CAN YOU POSSIBLY KNOW THESE THINGS!? And yes, the Earth is round."

"*Wooooaaaah....*"

Ami's eyes widened with wonder. He then squished his face in apparent concentration.

"*So...so if I swim in a straight line for a really really really long time, I'll come back to where I started? LET'S DO IT!*"

Suddenly, he started to swim away.

"No, Ami! Wait!" Lizzie was surprised to find that this apparent departure upset her; she liked this new friend! Talking with him was strangely what she needed...she didn't want him to go, not just yet...

"*What's up?*"

"Can we…can we talk some more please?"

"*Awwwh!*" Ami beamed and became bubblier than ever upon realizing that he meant something to this newfound terrestrial oddity. "*Of course we can talk some more!*"

He swam back, and they resumed conversation. For hours they went back and forth, asking each what it was like to be the other.

"So wait, you can see things that are invisible? That's amazing!"

"*Well, kind of, I need to get really close to it, but yeah! If there's a sneaky-sneaky fish hiding in the sand, I can pretty much feel where he is even if I can't see or smell him! Cool, huh?*"

"Way cool"

"*You know what else is cool? Hands!*"

"Well, I guess so"

"No, seriously dude! You can grab things without killing them! That's a gift...I try to carry things in my mouth sometimes, but it really doesn't go so well..."

Lizzie (who always had a bit of a darker side to humor) burst out laughing.

"Oh my gosh, Ami...." she calmed herself to an infectious giggle. "You're a goober. Also, why do you call me 'dude' all the time?"

"Uhhh...Lizzie, aren't you a dude? Like I'm a shark, you're a dude?"

"Bahaha!"

She happily corrected this error. They kept on talking in this way—bouncing from silly topic to silly topic—until the sun began to set, and Lizzie realized she had to leave.

"Ami, I have to go…" she began. She felt bittersweet; she was sad to leave this warm, wonderful strangeness, but counted herself fortunate to have ever experienced it in the first place.

"That's ok, I gotta grab dinner anyway." He seemed eager to hunt, but he too enjoyed this time with 'Lizzie Brock Who's Not a Dude'.

"Um, as long as you don't swim across the earth, can we meet up again?"

"Of course! I'd really, really like that!"

"I would too"

She smiled, and he smiled back as awkwardly as before. She hoped this was all not a dream.

"Ok, Ami" she got up, adjusted herself, and stared out into the falling sun.

This was really nice.

She turned down to her new little friend in the water.

"I'll see you tomorrow, ok? When the sun comes up"

"*No prob, Bob!*"

"How do you—never mind" she laughed and turned for home.

"*Goodbye*!" he called, and swam off into the deep.

"Goodbye" she muttered…she hoped this was not a dream…

The next day, Lizzie wandered back to the dock, and Amicus was there.

The sun came up.

Respect the seas and all who call them home.

~ *Thanks* ~

"To Lauren Jones and Hayley Brock, who are champions of friendship for being the sweetest, sassiest, shortest, most beautifully stupendous buddies whom I have been lucky enough to call 'friend'. You have a special place in my heart, and your cookies are always appreciated. ☺

To Andy Murch, who possesses a plethora of powerful photos at Elasmodiver.com; thank you for your stunning shot of Carcharhinus plumbeus (page 21). It made all the difference.

To those who have a dream; however grand it is, however impossible it seems, NEVER GIVE UP! Only YOU can seize destiny, and only YOU can hold yourself back. Keep seeking your higher self, and never let go of your love. "

~Zachary W. Nicholls
the First Dr. Jaws